The Rise and Fall of the Sacred Tree
& other collected poems

Jason Zadrozny

First Published on AKD Publishing in Great Britain in 2024

Complete Content Copyright Jason Zadrozny, 2024.

The right of Jason Zadrozny to be identified as the Author of the Work has been asserted by them in accordance with the Copyright, Designs and Patents Act 1988.

All rights reserved. No part of this publication may be reproduced, stored in a retrieval system, or transmitted in and form or by any means without prior written consent of the author, nor be otherwise circulated in any form or binding or cover other than that in which it is published and without a similar condition being imposed on the subsequent purchaser.

Copyright © 2024 Jason Zadrozny

All rights reserved.

ISBN: 9798338308844

THE RISE AND FALL OF THE SACRED TREE

DEDICATION

This book is dedicated to the one who saved me in every way a person can be saved. Thank you.

CONTENTS

Introduction

1	Pt 1: The Seraphs' Sacrilege.	Pg 1
2	Pt 2: Defiance And The Celestial Revenge.	Pg 6
3	Pt 3: The Fall Of The Sacred Tree.	Pg 16
4	Pt 4: The Age Of Reverence.	Pg 26
5	Pt 5: The Glimmer Of Redemption.	Pg 34
6	Pt 6: Epilogue: The Seraph's Final Lesson.	Pg 43

Poetry Anthology

7	The Cold Waking Wind Of The Night	Pg 48
8	Digging With David	Pg 51
9	Tim-e	Pg 54
10	Blood In A Snowstorm	Pg 56
11	Froggatt Edge Stone Circle	Pg 58
12	Endings	Pg 60
13	Black Panther	Pg 62
14	M40	Pg 64
15	Just Past Ten	Pg 66

THE RISE AND FALL OF THE SACRED TREE

16	Another Morn	Pg 68
17	Nightmare!	Pg 70
18	Enchanting Mutiny	Pg 71
19	My Sweet Confessor	Pg 73
20	Just Alone	Pg 76
21	What Can I See?	Pg 77
22	Death's Legacy	Pg 79
23	Distance	Pg 81
24	Cold Steel	Pg 84
25	Solemness	Pg 86
26	Guide To A Grith	Pg 87
27	Realisation Of Blindness	Pg 89
28	The Awakening To The Promised Land	Pg 91
29	Could It Be!	Pg 95
30	Angel Face	Pg 97
31	Who	Pg 98
32	The Grace Of The Gun Guise	Pg 100
33	To Become	Pg 102
34	Gyratory Potential	Pg 103
35	Thinking Of You	Pg 105

THE RISE AND FALL OF THE SACRED TREE

36	And Love	Pg 107
37	Hunger	Pg 108
38	Know Where I'm Going?	Pg 109
39	Tormented Time	Pg 111
40	Speaking In An Accent	Pg 113
41	Dusty Sunset	Pg 115
42	Tired Hands	Pg 116
43	Coming Home	Pg 117
44	Star-drenched Thunder	Pg 119
45	Please Think of Me	Pg 121
46	Secrets Of The Dark	Pg 123
47	Watery Eyes	Pg 125
48	Days, Days, Days	Pg 127
49	Perspective	Pg 129
50	P.O.W.	Pg 134
51	Lies	Pg 136
52	An Ode To A Distant Memory	Pg 138
53	Yesterday Was A Long Time Ago	Pg 142
54	Tomorrows Trepidation	Pg 144
55	Opposite Toad's Mouth	Pg 145

56	From The Crossbeam	Pg 147
57	Coughing	Pg 150
58	The Tale The Tree Could Have Told	Pg 152
59	The Unknown	Pg 155
60	A Friend In Need	Pg 159
61	Melancholy Mother	Pg 161
62	Fruit For Thought	Pg 163
63	The Mirror Of Truth	Pg 165
64	October The Second, Nineteen Hundred and Ninety-Nie	Pg 167
65	A Face In The Mud	Pg 168
66	Anchored In The Rain	Pg 170
67	Words Of Worth	Pg 172
68	The Demon's Duty	Pg 174
69	Citizen Z	Pg 176

INTRODUCTION

This book, a labour of love spanning over 25 years, is the culmination of a journey that began in the depths of youthful imagination and has been nurtured through decades of reflection and growth.

The epic poem you hold in your hands is not merely a work of fiction, but a meditation on the forces that shape our world - forces as ancient as time and as urgent as the present moment.

At its core, this epic poem is a rich tapestry of themes that weave together the sacred and the profane, the past and the future, the divine and the earthly. It is a story of creation and destruction, of pride and redemption, of nature's enduring grace and humanity's fragile relationship with it.

Through its verses, I have sought to explore the profound consequences of mankind's choices - how our reverence for the sacred can easily give way to hubris, and how our connection to the earth, once a source of life, can become a path to desolation if neglected.

The symbolism within this poem is both overt and subtle, drawing heavily from religious history, mythology, and environmental awareness. The tree, central to the narrative, is not just a symbol of life and growth, but also of knowledge, temptation, and the cyclical nature of existence. It stands as a testament to humanity's initial reverence for the divine and natural world, a reverence that slowly erodes over time, giving way to greed and industrial ambition. The tree's transformation from a source of light and hope to a harbinger of darkness and despair mirrors our own trajectory as a species - how we have moved from worshipping the natural world to exploiting it, often with disastrous consequences.

This poem also delves deeply into the realms of religious history and mythology, drawing inspiration from the rich traditions of angelic hierarchies, divine battles, and the timeless struggle between good and evil. The Seraph, the Archangel, and the celestial council are not just characters in a story, but embodiments of the eternal conflict between light and dark, faith and doubt, creation and destruction. Their struggles are mirrored in the earthly realm, where mankind's choices resonate with cosmic significance.

My passion for history - particularly religious history - has been a guiding force throughout the creation of this work. The poem is imbued with the echoes of ancient texts, the wisdom of the ancients, and the moral quandaries that have been debated for millennia. Yet, it is also a contemporary work, reflecting the environmental concerns that have become increasingly urgent in our time. The destruction of the tree and the subsequent desolation of the earth serve as a powerful allegory for the environmental degradation we witness today, a warning of what may come if we do not heed the lessons of the past.

Over the years, I have returned to this poem time and again, each time adding new layers, new insights, and new reflections. It has been a constant companion, growing and evolving with me as I have grown and evolved. This work has been a refuge in times of doubt, a challenge in times of complacency, and a joy in times of inspiration.

The poem is not just a story - it is a meditation, a prayer, and a call to action. It is my hope that as you read these verses, you will be transported to the realms of the divine and the earthly, where the choices we make reverberate through time and space, shaping the world for generations to come. May it inspire you to reflect on our shared history, our fragile environment, and the enduring power of hope, love, and redemption.

The other collected works are an eclectic anthology of poetry that spans years of reflection and emotional depths. Written in a variety of styles, this compilation captures the essence of youthful passion, vulnerability, and introspection. Written over a quarter of a century ago, while I was at the end of my teenage years. From moments of intense joy, the imagination of desolation, to quiet contemplation, each poem offers a glimpse into the raw and ever-changing landscape of youthful emotions.

Whether you are seeking solace, inspiration, or connection, these whispers through time invite readers on a timeless journey through the universal experiences of growth, love, and self-discovery.

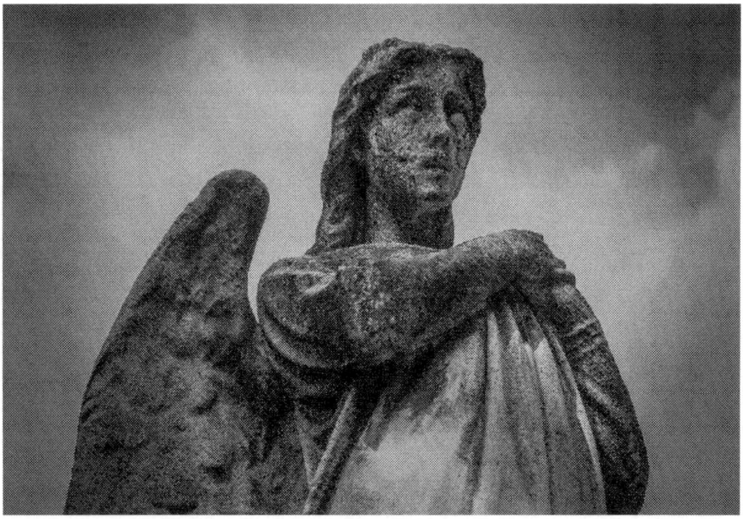

1 THE SERAPHS' SACRILEGE

Entertaining his bones with a muscled dance.

He stops, occasionally, on the beat to glance

nonchalantly, imperturbably, at the crowd.

Who melt around his wings; a pale-faced cloud.

He glides like a swan with limbs as light,

he darts like a firefly – blindingly bright.

He slices the air as sharp as a knife,

drunk on the lust of both power and life.

He falters and trips, he trips, he screams.

Burnt to his roots: the mask from his dreams.

His eyes burst with fire, his now ashen face

hazily gleaming. Tumbling from grace.

THE RISE AND FALL OF THE SACRED TREE

Wrought in his dream time, the mask dissolves.

Etching, corroding - an imprint evolves.

An imprint encroaching, fashioned of night.

Beckons him wraithlike and plucks out his sight.

As shadows engulf him, cold fingers grip,

each breath a struggle, each step a slip.

The crowd recoils, their pale faces white,

as the Seraph descends into limitless night.

That night becomes day. The moon falls from view.

The tepid sun rises and freezes the dew.

The sun much too pale to deliver his sight,

allotting mere shadows to assist him in plight.

THE RISE AND FALL OF THE SACRED TREE

The room that was, is there no more.

Stripped to the atom; stripped to the core.

The onlookers too, in the snap of a flash:

emaciated, ignited, cremated to ash.

The horizon reforms, but nothing is there

the landscape has altered, akin to the air.

An eternal desert, with ice-grains for sand.

The wind fills with rime: he proffers his hand.

He musters his soul; he forms a flame,

to sit in his hand and warm through his shame.

He can't burn his soul for heat anymore,

he pours to his knees and scrabbles the floor.

THE RISE AND FALL OF THE SACRED TREE

Fingers scrape cold, the frost clinging tight,

desperation echoing in the still of night.

The heavens remain, distant and bleak,

no whispers of solace, no guidance to seek.

The ground is fruitless, as frosted as pride.

Ignorant to his indigence: austerity doth chide.

The sleet-sodden air, beginning to churn,

plucks out his feathers. He grabs them to burn.

The plumage he burns to make the flames grow,

heats up his anger and so melts the snow.

The arctic reign gone, the ice fields no more.

He darts toward heaven to alter the score.

THE RISE AND FALL OF THE SACRED TREE

Colossal ramparts enclose his goal.

Their fortifications shoulder no hole.

Iridescent, irregular, ice-fall blue:

the floes bind iniquity: an unyielding glue.

Cherubim peer through the liquid cage,

a fantastic might summoned with rage.

The celestial hierarchy prepares their defense,

certain in heart what is sure to commence.

2 DEFIANCE AND THE CELESTIAL REVENGE

Resembling Moses: sculpting the sea,

the Seraph stabs stings at the walls like a bee.

Now God does not fill his glaive any longer,

the Seraph, sagacious, views which is stronger.

His once-proud weapons fall hollow and weak,

forbidden to wield the power he seeks.

His fury now spent, his soul stands bare,

before the watchful eyes that no longer care.

The archaic wisdom draws open the gate.

The Seraph hauled in by a tempest of hate.

Hurled back to Earth: The Thrones' choir sings

as the breath of The Lord shreds off his wings.

THE RISE AND FALL OF THE SACRED TREE

THE RISE AND FALL OF THE SACRED TREE

His body lies limply on the baked arid soil.

His wounds bubble blood; he comes to the boil.

Breath steams out into the cracking parched air,

the Seraph screams dryly; a vengeance-soaked prayer.

In the desert's expanse, the heavens are still,

no answer, no mercy, no offering of will.

He writhes in a torment, his soul set alight,

a fallen star burns in vast endless night.

The gaping gashes seal up in a slice.

A smooth mustard skin wraps tight its vice.

The viscous shell, that plugs his hurt, spreads.

Vine-like it creeps. The soft magma treads.

Twisting and binding, his form now anew,

a grotesque cocoon, where torment imbues.

His limbs retract, his figure deforms,

the once-mighty Seraph now writhes and conforms.

Fusing his bones and melting his skin,

the scars swallow fast: encasing him in

a fat tube of tissue. Pulsating, sliding –

the new grub folds: shrinking, hiding.

A rapid autolytic cycle proceeds,

shrivelling him down to the level of seeds.

A giant world now, bitter and tart,

where benevolent hearts are much further apart.

THE RISE AND FALL OF THE SACRED TREE

As he diminishes, the world grows vast,

a shadow of grandeur, a memory passed.

The skies remain distant, a bleak, solemn dome,

no place for the Seraph, no refuge or home.

A rumble above, the clouds shift their place;

fading in colour and gathering pace.

A rupture appears, The Thrones' chorus sings:

down from the clouds drift the late Seraph's wings.

Perished and putrid the rotten wings rest.

A contagion within and this was God's jest.

From high in the heavens Jove watched in wait:

to witness the maggot seizing the bait.

THE RISE AND FALL OF THE SACRED TREE

The stench of decay blockades the cold air,

a scent of finality, a pure divine snare.

The Seraph, once proud, drawn right to the rot,

a reflection of all the power he sought.

The larva to whom the wings had belonged,

edged toward them, not knowing he'd wronged.

Filled up with emptiness, starving for food,

he ate the corruption – feeding the feud.

Gorging guiltlessly the grub feeds on flesh.

Gobbling a path through the sinewy mesh.

Brimming with pus: he resurfaces, content.

He bathes in the clemency and reflects no repent.

THE RISE AND FALL OF THE SACRED TREE

A fledgling Jackdaw that's fleeting by,

sights the pupa in its juvenile eye.

It dives with the skill of a stone thrown in joy,

ladling the shape in its beak like a toy.

Transporting it's cargo above the stones,

like fruit around kernels; as flesh covers bones.

It carries the gem over now brutal sea.

Then splutters on nought and coughs the bud free.

The bud drips through calmness, sinking slow,

like the lightest of flecks of the spongy deft snow.

Twisting through sky he falls through the clouds,

the air coalescing around him in shrouds.

THE RISE AND FALL OF THE SACRED TREE

The arrow shape punctures a placid lake skin,

Its mirror-like surface swathing him in

a world of cold bubbles, glassy and clear;

a blinding translucence – throbbing with fear.

Lining the bottom of a gravelly bed,

the husk sits firmly, carmine and red.

To the bank he then drifts, an effortless hike:

nudged by the nose of a wandering pike.

Discarded on the frame of the claret tarn,

the form unravels from its encasing yarn.

With a burst of release the shell starts to quake,

from out of the casing a beetle doth break.

THE RISE AND FALL OF THE SACRED TREE

Scurrying around, both shiny and new.

He discovers a spider and breaks it to chew.

He sucks out the juice from its split hollow legs,

he opens the stomach and feeds on its eggs.

He exits the carcass, he looks to the sky,

his eyes become cloudlike, milky and dry.

The beetle squats sluggishly, rapt from the heat.

The sun starts to desiccate, congealing his meat.

Solidified and still he dries to the bone,

perched on the shore, rebuffed and alone.

Twigs that were limbs, now harden and fall,

the seed stands defiantly, tiny yet tall.

The sands of time pass, their sediment forms.

Buried in history the musing seed warms.

An influx of vim; a new life to live,

goodness to take yet sourness to give.

Its volume increases; its area grows,

rippling and heaving its root system flows.

The shoot expands outwards, out of the ground,

its crawlers undulating: traversing the mound.

Swollen with pride, the tree stands resolved.

On a platform of hillside: where life had dissolved.

It looms in the distance of everyone's view,

beckoning with coyness; inviting and new.

3 THE FALL OF THE SACRED TREE

In the barren waste, the tree stands grim,

its once proud visage, worn now and dim.

Roots that once delved into soils thus deep,

now pulse with a blight, in a hew poisoned sleep.

Molten rock swallows the trunk as charred bark,

a searing-flamed curse in the desolate dark.

Twisting vines, sharp and ignited,

Wrap 'round its trunk, ill, cursed and blighted.

No verdant leaves, no life to glean,

only deformed forms in a macabre scene.

The fruits it bears, a blood-red-like stain,

drip venomous nectar, a scarlet death bane.

THE RISE AND FALL OF THE SACRED TREE

THE RISE AND FALL OF THE SACRED TREE

Beneath the red glow, creatures draw near,

their eyes glazed with hunger, devoid of all fear.

They gnaw at the bark, they drink of that bane,

their once-bright souls turned cavernous pain.

Ravens descend, their caws sharp and clear,

pecking at flesh that the tree still holds dear.

They fight for the marrow, the mold rotting core,

while the tree exudes darkness, cursed evermore?

Dark as night, the dew that falls,

each drop a curse, each sip enthralls.

Creatures gather; their hunger deep set.

to feast on the fruit, their hearts no regret.

THE RISE AND FALL OF THE SACRED TREE

They gnash, they tear, they consume with glee,

Unaware of devouring what once was born free.

Their eyes glaze sour, their souls fall ensnared,

In the tree's dark shadow, they're drowned and impaired.

The Seraph, now a gnarled, woven tree,

Watches, in waiting, for his green soul set free.

His laughter echoes, hollow and cold,

vowless, canorous, evil, and old.

The heavens tremble, pausing their breath

as corruption spreads, seeking new death.

The Thrones and Cherubim take firm their stand,

to cleanse the torment that scourges the land.

THE RISE AND FALL OF THE SACRED TREE

A council constructed, a proposal is made,

a warrior chosen, sagely afraid.

Archangel Michael, holding God's blade of light,

is sent to bring just to the mad Seraph's blight.

From the heights of heaven, Michael descends,

through realms of fire where nought ever bends.

His wings aflame with righteous might,

carving through shadows, dispersing the night.

Through sick warped lands, the Angel strides,

fronting horrors where darkness hides.

The path is fraught with nightmare dreams,

Where reality unravels, and there it seems -

THE RISE AND FALL OF THE SACRED TREE

memories of a brother's loss,

of the Seraph's fall - the highest cost.

Yet still the Angel presses on,

to see the damned tree undone.

Each step he takes ignites the earth,

purging the blight with divine rebirth.

The ground groans, furies beneath his feet,

as hellish flames from below bid retreat.

At the root of the tree, the Angel stands,

holy blade grasped in celestial hands.

Distorted spectres start swarming like flies,

their ghostly wails, the deafening cries.

THE RISE AND FALL OF THE SACRED TREE

The battle rages, dark against light,

the Angel's blade slashes, tearing the night.

Each strike a beacon, each swing a flare,

Piercing the veil of hate and despair.

The tree itself begins to writhe,

its roots lashing out, a strong serpent's scythe.

The Seraph's voice booms, with venom it's laced,

taunting the Angel with now fallen grace.

"You think me vanquished, you think me weak?"

The Seraph's voice hissing, frozen and bleak.

"You are too late, the infection is sown.

In my defeat, your end will be shown."

THE RISE AND FALL OF THE SACRED TREE

The Angel's heart persists steadfast and pure,

his resolve like iron, his force will endure.

He pierces through the tempestuous night,

a luminous flame, burning emerald bright.

The holy blade is immersed deeply within,

the whole tree shudders, roots growing thin.

Poisonous flames crumble to ash and to dust,

the Seraph cries out, a thunderous gust.

The tree fractures, beginning to fall,

Its branches shatter, its roots cease their crawl.

The Seraph screams, a pitched final plea,

as his spirit unravels, setting him free.

THE RISE AND FALL OF THE SACRED TREE

The ground quakes, the sky turning pale,

the darkness lifts, the west winds exhale.

The embittered land begins to heal,

as light reappears, bright, sharp, and real.

The Angel stands, his mission is done,

the battle is fought, the victory won.

Creatures freed from a torturous bind,

their souls released, their peace they do find.

A glowing seed, now all that remains,

of the Seraph's timber, malevolent chains.

The Angel plants it, deeply and sure,

in sacred soils, unpolluted and pure.

THE RISE AND FALL OF THE SACRED TREE

A new tree grows, a symbol bright,

of redemption's power, of hope, of light.

The heavens sing, the stars align,

a tale of grace through times divine.

4 THE AGE OF REVERENCE

The tree grew tall, a benevolent beacon,

its roots intertwined with the heart none could weaken.

A temple arose, carved from pure stone,

where people would gather - their sins to atone.

Beneath its branches, they prayed, and they sang,

their voices echoed, where spirits would hang.

The fruits of the tree, again rubies red,

were taken as blessings, and life newly fed.

Pilgrims travelled from lands near and far,

to bask in the glow of the tree's trusting star.

They brought their offerings, their hopes, and their dreams,

trusting the power that flowed from its seams.

THE RISE AND FALL OF THE SACRED TREE

Less the tree's shade, life now did bloom,

no soul left untouched by its jasmine perfume.

The land befell lush, a garden serene,

a testament of where Jove's angels had been.

Marriages were blessed, newborns were kissed,

under the boughs where the soft breezes hissed.

The dead were laid down, reposed in holy light,

their spirits entwined in roots of night.

Seasons flowed with abundance and pace,

the land a paradise, an all-hallowed space.

The skies were clear, the rains fell right,

and all lived in harmony and bathed in the light.

THE RISE AND FALL OF THE SACRED TREE

Time's cruel hand began to memories erode.

The tale of the tree turned an aged, faded ode.

Faith that flourished, now weakened breath thin,

what once was most sacred, just the dream of a hymn.

Men turned to machines, to steel and hot fire,

their hearts oft consumed by relentless desire.

The temple decayed, ruined pillars cracked,

the worshippers gone, their footsteps untracked.

The tree stood abandoned in a world made of stone,

its whispers of wisdom by the storm overblown.

Forests were felled, coarse rivers were tamed,

nature's pure beauty, so ruthlessly maimed.

THE RISE AND FALL OF THE SACRED TREE

The tree became naught but a relic of lore,

an obstacle now in the path of the poor.

Its roots once revered, torn from the earth,

its leaves that once healed, crushed without worth.

The boughs that lunged high for the stars up above,

were chopped down then burned, devoid now of love.

Eventually, came the day when the proud tree would fall,

mankind's ambition swallowed grief's final call.

The saws bit deep, the bark split wide,

the sacred giant, humbled by pride.

The very earth trembled, the sky curdled grey,

as the ancient one fell, its life giving way.

THE RISE AND FALL OF THE SACRED TREE

The flames were kindled, the wood stacked high,

the once mighty tree gave to fire and sky.

Smoke rose thick, a bleak shroud of night,

Blotting the sun with its venomous blight.

The essence of ages, corrupted and fouled,

ascended to heaven where angels now howled.

In the realm above, where the angels flew,

the smoke of the tree choked the heavens to blue.

Light grew dim, their wings grew weak,

their voices fell silent, too choked to speak.

One by one, they faltered and died,

their halos extinguished, grace cast aside.

THE RISE AND FALL OF THE SACRED TREE

The songs of the spheres became echoes of pain,

as the smoke fetched in death, a fate-darkened stain.

The Thrones, the Cherubs, the Seraphim too,

were lost to this wind like a drop of warm dew.

The heavens lay empty, cold and bereft,

no guardians endured, no protectors were left.

Below on earth, the world fast was changed,

the balance was shattered, the seasons deranged.

Storms thundered wild, the oceans made rise,

as mankind looked on with dread in their eyes.

Crops fail, life halts, and rivers run dry,

sickness and misery spread under the sky.

THE RISE AND FALL OF THE SACRED TREE

No comfort was found, no hope up ahead,

for the angels were gone, the tree's love was dead.

In the shadow of progress, a wasteland bred,

a world without colour, empty and dead.

The smoke had ascended, the heavens had choked,

and mankind was left with the hell they'd invoked.

The trees ashy snowstorm fled far, scattering wide,

trickled by winds across every divide.

Where once there was life - pervasive despair,

for mankind had spent what was precious and rare.

This was a portent, a counsel to see,

of the cost of man's greed, not just of the tree.

THE RISE AND FALL OF THE SACRED TREE

Turning from nature, we sever the thread,

we find only darkness, and all light is dead.

The world now spins in a half-silent scream,

a ghost of its past, a sad elapsed dream.

The tree that once flourished, now dust in the breeze,

and mankind, alone, dropped to its knees.

The heavens, still, silent, offer man no reply,

as the world fades hastily, under calm deepened sky.

This tale of pride, of fall, of grace,

a warning etched in time and space.

For those who listen, who heed its call,

there may yet be hope, though shadows do fall.

5 THE GLIMMER OF REDEMPTION

Yet as the heavens lie glacial and bare,

the stars still obscured by a smoky snare,

mankind wanders through shadows vast,

haunted by echoes of a once glorious past.

The Angels' song, now a silent dirge,

leaving mortal souls on the brink, on a verge

where hope seems but a detached dream,

drowned far below desire's glass stream.

The earth, through scars, softly still breathes,

with ancient whispering between new formed leaves.

Her bones, the mountains; her bloodflow, the sea,

the cradle of life, eternally free.

THE RISE AND FALL OF THE SACRED TREE

THE RISE AND FALL OF THE SACRED TREE

Yet now she quivers, saps weary and worn,

her forests are razed, her meadows ripped, torn.

Except in her veins, a faint pulse persists,

a gentle rhythm, of lifeblood's last tryst.

Amidst the ruins, a subtle shrill sound,

a murmur, faint, from within sacred ground.

The roots still hold though the tree has withdrawn,

a reminder that life's thread yet still could spawn.

For though the angels have perished, lying still,

some sparks still smoulder, raged against will.

A reminder waking, from dust, we rise,

found in the earth, our true strength there lies.

THE RISE AND FALL OF THE SACRED TREE

O man, who falters, absorbed in the night,

blinded by greed's all insatiable blight,

O man, who falters, consumed by such greed,

can you not see what your soul doth need?

Can you not feel the earth's torn lament?

The sorrow of a world, entrusted, misspent?

Not treasure nor might, ephemeral, profane,

but generosity and blessings to mollify the strain.

Within that sorrow, a pit there does lie,

awaiting the tears that weep from the sky.

Tears of repentance, of newborn clement grace,

to nourish the soil, untarnish disgrace.

THE RISE AND FALL OF THE SACRED TREE

If we, in humility, learn to tread,

with lightened hearts where darkness spread,

to turn from the path, that led to this waste,

and embrace the virtues we've long displaced —

there, in the furrows of a fallow land,

might spring forth blossoms, by a gentle hand.

For love, once buried, can rise anew,

like a phoenix from the ash, from coals, and from dew.

The earth, our home, though battered and torn,

still cradles life, and each new day born.

Her hills, though now hollowed, still hum with sound,

of winds that weave throughout the sacred ground.

THE RISE AND FALL OF THE SACRED TREE

If we but listen, with an open ear,

to the silent hymns that once we held dear,

perhaps we'll find, in that ancient brave song,

the strength to right what has fallen so wrong.

Though greed has spread its cankered root,

and choked the tree that bore sweet fruit,

there's yet a chance, a slender reed,

if we choose to suppose what our hearts truly need.

Not wealth, nor power, nor fleeting fame,

but love, hope, and charity, pure as his flame.

For even in this darkest hour,

there lies within all, a staunch latent power.

THE RISE AND FALL OF THE SACRED TREE

To turn the tide, to heal the breach,

to find in humility what pride cannot teach.

To cherish life, to mend what's torn,

to bring forth the dawn where the drear night was born.

And from the ashes of our past,

to forge a future sound will last.

Not built on stone, or steel, or gold,

but on the bonds, real love of old.

Let us, with reverence, handle the soil,

and with tender hands, undo the spoil.

To plant anew, with care and grace,

a garden where life has found again place.

THE RISE AND FALL OF THE SACRED TREE

For in the earth's embrace, we find,

the solace for our troubled mind.

And perhaps, just perhaps, in this sacred task,

we'll find the redemption for which we ask.

So let this lesson be our guide,

a beacon in the pitch-black tide.

For though the angels' light has dimmed,

and faith in man seems worn and trimmed,

there's yet a glimmer in the night,

a chance to make the injustices right.

If we but choose to walk with care,

to love, to hope, fix to repair.

THE RISE AND FALL OF THE SACRED TREE

From the seed of that self-effacing choice,

may rise a fresh and steadfast voice.

A song that echoes throughout the land,

a hymn of peace, and a gentle hand.

For though we've strayed, and lost our way,

the dawn still waits to acknowledge the day.

And in that understanding, so pure and bright,

may mankind find its guiding light.

6 EPILOGUE: THE SERAPH'S FINAL LESSON

The Seraph, in discernment, hid loyal deep,

had played his part, through mad trials steep.

For all this test, from first breath to last,

was a sacrifice hidden in hell's shadows cast.

He warped, he fell hard, earth potent did quake,

yet, was to stir man's soul - to break

the grip of ignorance, the mind ensnared,

so faith could flourish, a treasure declared.

In death's embrace, the Seraph lies still,

his once-perverse roots, calm now, tranquil.

For all his rage and his fury-filled fall,

A deeper truth held him, profoundly enthralled.

THE RISE AND FALL OF THE SACRED TREE

THE RISE AND FALL OF THE SACRED TREE

He warped the world, he fell from grace,

but in his ruin, truth found its real place.

For man and angel, both lost their way,

but in their loss, an intense light did stay.

The Seraph's fall, a sacrifice made,

to break the chains where shadows played.

His soul, once blackened, now shines anew,

a gleaming star in clear heaven's view.

For through his torment, through fire and hate,

the Seraph had played a role too great.

He stirred the earth, shook man to his core,

to bring them back, to faith in what's sure.

THE RISE AND FALL OF THE SACRED TREE

His spirit a raincloud, drifts through the air,

a sentinel of the world with caution and care.

His laughter, once hollow, now rich with grace,

a guardian, in waiting, for the whole human race.

And though he fell, through anguish and flame,

is legacy endures, eternal, untamed.

For in the ashes of his misshapen past,

a lesson of redemption will eternally last.

For in his fall, the lesson was plain:

to lose the divine is to court endless pain.

In his ruin, a covenant, holy restored –

in faith's true light, he found 'gain the Lord.

COLLECTED POEMS

THE RISE AND FALL OF THE SACRED TREE

THE COLD WAKING WIND OF THE NIGHT.

I saw you standing there again last night,

hidden amidst a hurricane of shadows.

Drifting in and out of sight,

my hopeful imagination searching for a bouquet of your brazen

affection.

Creative thoughts, saw you leaning over me in the dusky hours,

delivering a parcel of unique allure.

Silent and soft as a garden of flowers,

my upside-down conscience hesitates, pulling away from

mistakes made by an insecure heart.

Even dreams from heaven aren't this real,

as you cradle me in your arms.

Tormenting the choking isolation I feel,

as the cold shudder of you wakes me in the dead of night.

THE RISE AND FALL OF THE SACRED TREE

You appear, whispering soft melodies of love,

so close, my awaiting ear receives with them arousing gusts of

your warm breath.

With the presence and energy of a star from above,

can your slender ghost taunt me until fulfilment?

Even as difficult as it seems,

I touch you and long for you to touch me too.

But you fly to remain only in my dreams,

my eternal fantasy of love.

When I carefully open my eyes,

I can't believe that you make me feel so unhappily content.

Shuddering each time that I realise,

that you have evaporated with the darkened hours.

THE RISE AND FALL OF THE SACRED TREE

Will you return again tomorrow in the night,

when I'm stranded and yearning for you.

Stand again there, in the red firelight,

so, I may see you as you re-whisper loving words of cruel comfort.

THE RISE AND FALL OF THE SACRED TREE

DIGGING WITH DAVID.
(Inspired by Hecht's poem, "More light! More light!*)

In a line we stood all three,

digging for the last decree.

Fate unknown, we couldn't guess,

to the bowels of the earth, we dug,

a fate unseen from the gentle SS,

the wet smooth mud under like a rug.

A rifle pointed from the back,

ordered them, to lie in our gauged-out track.

Reason, yellow stars with equal points,

they quivered slightly from fear and frost,

unquestioned death, on them, anoints,

hope dislodged or maybe just lost.

I was told to cover them with the soil,

which was the work of their disheartened toil.

Slowly I obeyed until I reached their eyes,

full of briny tears and such sorrow,

to know they would be food for flies,

when they were dead by morrow.

The last spade full, I held my breath,

covered them and confirmed their tragic death.

Maybe the stars plumped upon their chest,

used by them to convey peace and love,

would help them always steadily rest,

when they reached their skies above.

THE RISE AND FALL OF THE SACRED TREE

I knew that I could only find,

a certain, true, calm peace of mind.

When from behind, the rifles lead,

would send me down to hell,

and pierce me through hair and skull and head,

an unrested soul, with Satan to dwell.

TIM-E.

Grey twinned sheep, thin wool clinging to your young chest.

Deep welling caramel eyes - full of surprise, and filled with brimming buckets of diluted brine.

Your brother feels your secret pain - but dare not ask to gain, the knowledge of what you dare not tell him.

So, he will peer patiently out, from under his labelled peaked cap. Protected from the notion of losing you.

He is crushed by the fear - that he may steer you away if you cannot tell him, the revelation he has already learned.

Yet wordless you stay - hoping that if you say nothing at all, you can keep him and your sibling security.

THE RISE AND FALL OF THE SACRED TREE

Brotherly bonds burn while trying to be held together by hot hands - release them and reforge thicker chains of love through trusting openness.

You can't run or hide forever - for deep inside you somewhere, the alkaline of time drips droplets of corrosive complacency, on your individual furrow of thought.

Then when canker blossoms in your perfectly pretended pasture, you will not only look like a little imitation lamb – but you will follow like one.

15. February 1999.

THE RISE AND FALL OF THE SACRED TREE

BLOOD IN A SNOWSTORM.

Fragile thin flakes swirl in a cold funnel of wind.

I stand in the storm's eye and watch, watch them chasing each other. Pushing the night sky's roundabout faster and faster.

Dizzily and wearily they fade their speed, pause on a gust, then glide gracefully to the ground. Appearing like expiring paper airplanes, perishing towards the pavement.

Unblemished unsullied innocents, instantly contaminated by the grimy majestic squalor. Then are veiled lugubriously, by the loathsome immersion in impure pollution. Molested by the mucky mud.

Blood billows out, brought about by their beating.

Shrill yelps scream out sharply, the tale of savage, sinful, spite.

Prevalent oaths coil with mastery around the tongues of odious observants. Confirming a ballot of boorish phantoms, who with foresight and sagacity, dispense animated absorbents to soak up the sorrowful substandard snow.

Only the snows have vanished, and all they leave in their place are wild, woeful, wet watery tears.

25. February 1999.

THE RISE AND FALL OF THE SACRED TREE
FROGGATT EDGE STONE CIRCLE.

Gnarled twisted bracken stands like fudge-coloured spears, shooting up though broken, from the porous squelching soil.

The wind blows cold whistles over half drunken bottles of thirst relevant, and her merry tune bedazzles the mind. So then we forget how icy her snow-flecked breezes really are.

Frozen fingers tap to the melody of her conducted orchestral fluting.

Then you see the stones sitting patiently in a circle, and waiting for you to arrive.

Thick generous moss reforms the embarking cracks, with its make better mosaics.

The stones greet by joining the winds chorus, with a sentimental song of their own.

Noble myths are they, proud among the fells, breaking the skyline with their stately significance.

Aged neglected ornaments erupted upon the landscape, adorning habitual grasses.

Flooding moors with conquering energy, defeating distress and subdue the senses, leaving only heartily promises.

Amid astounding airs, only affection and endearment can touch the emotions

ENDINGS.

Dawn began breaking, yet she did not stir,

For the midst of the night had faded with her.

She died all alone, in her bed, in the night,

Slipped away daintily and resisted the fight.

Cocooned in her bedclothes, still warm and soft,

She bided farewell as she gazed from aloft.

The nets on the window whispered a wheeze,

As they danced in the dawn, on the gust of a breeze.

Letters were posted never to be read,

By the pale, sullen eyes, that now were quite dead.

Milk bottles chinked as they stood on the stair,

Placed without knowing that she wasn't there.

THE RISE AND FALL OF THE SACRED TREE

Her body lay still, her skin milky white,

Stained by the moon in the dead of the night.

Family would miss her, and tears would fall,

As they cradled the cat on the chair in the hall.

And no one would forget her, her memory strong,

Her smiling pink face in the cheer of a song.

But none could express in the words that they'd say,

It was in that night that our world passed away.

BLACK PANTHER.

Through the fluorescent neon jungle,

I watch you stroll.

A vast city, now fallen, is your home, and where a stout tree

replaces a fallen fourth column I see you pad through – a jewel.

You curl in a patch of white sunlight – mauling your third prey

in twenty minutes.

Smiling, curvaceous, ignorant of your worth.

Blonde curls fall easily from your jade coat.

Then you lick your claws and free them from the flavour rested

in the grain.

Roll and relax on your back, lifting the steamed carcass and

allow the remaining morsels to drain out into your gaping jaw.

THE RISE AND FALL OF THE SACRED TREE

Catch my eye and smile again – unknowingly.

Again jagged flashes flicker in your view,

And off you move,

Meandering through the musical laughter – restless in one place.

The Crowned Prince of a private principality.

Soft black panther, sleek and seductive,

Dark and dangerous,

Lovely yet lethal.

Never to be understood.

Never to be owned.

Always to be wanted.

M40.

I feel sure I'm supposed to be happy now,

Everyone is happy for me.

Is this my only go at it all?

Don't I get a run-through, a final dress rehearsal?

Just to iron out the creases – I do want to get it right.

Perhaps I can scribble it all out, start again. Rewind and rerecord,

or just show the edited highlights.

I feel sure I'm supposed to be happy now.

It's all going to come together, they say,

like cake mixture.

Only I'm frightened of missing an ingredient or burning it and ruining it altogether.

I feel sure I'm supposed to be happy now.

THE RISE AND FALL OF THE SACRED TREE

I dug out an old canvas, to paint on.

Can't afford a new one, this will do,

I'll blank it out first and then start.

Whitewash – clean away all of the old stuff.

Then paint on the new… in anticipation.

I hope it dries quickly,

I've seen it smudged before.

I feel sure I'm supposed to be happy - now.

28 March 2000

JUST PAST TEN.

The watermark of darkness stains the light in the room.

A broad and a slender shaft of light spear through the heavy damask drapes. Resting easily on the curvature of the ceiling – amber and unpolished.

Eager impatient gusts of steady wind gallop by, creaking occasionally. Moaning once, about the cold.

For the cold has encapsulated everything in a timeless pause.

Frozen the whistle over the reeds, the midnight mending of a flapping web and the wheezing breath of a nervous insomniac.

Cemented in a reversed turban of blankets, I listen but hear nought – save twitching beams and panes grown old.

THE RISE AND FALL OF THE SACRED TREE

I hold out my ear daintily, hoping for the sound of the ten o'clock horses – but too much of the eclipse has passed for them to come.

Saddling another storm are they, on burnished pressed leather – riding the wayward winds.

Brine form the melting clouds, canters by in their place, unpure, unpure and filthed with grime.

Tether the nights of peace on my slumber and wake me only when the ten o'clock horses are riding near.

I have a cube of sugar for the blackest one.

ANOTHER MORN.

My only companion was lonesomeness,

I've tried to mask it from them all.

My brain scrambles thoughts into such a mess,

that I'm too weak to let out a call.

Words spear my throat, as would a dagger.

Fooling people with a cleaver guise,

Then crying in the dark.

Telling everyone so many lies,

living life with an unlit spark.

Oblivion from any happiness.

THE RISE AND FALL OF THE SACRED TREE

Things turn out as a difficult game,

why should I keep on trying?

When inside I'm still the same,

and feel as though I'm dying.

Torn fiercely from the inside, out.

A tear will fall and slowly break,

when heartstrings become too worn.

Then, I'll hope not to awake,

to absorb the pain of another morn.

Dreams of sensational calm, perhaps.

12 October 1998

THE RISE AND FALL OF THE SACRED TREE

NIGHTMARE !

'Twas dark,

    'twas stormy,

        'twas dead of night!

My heart, it pounded! Full of fright.

Sat quiet,

    sat still,

        no breath from fear,

When of a sudden, did ghosts appear.

At foot of bed,

    they were stood,

cloaked in black, in cape and hood.

Each took a limb, pulled out my life,

My soul to death, by kitchen knife.

Yelled and screamed, but awoke next morn,

With day of spring, for to adorn.

31 October 1998

ENCHANTING MUTINY.

How honest is the forest glade,

that lies unstirred and as God made.

What truth will hide beneath the twigs,

and through the roots where badger digs.

Their course-weaved net disguises the sadness below.

The soil and sand, still precious land,

is churned and moulded more,

into a fatal beauty, of which we must adore.

Should you be grateful for the single tree left mighty?

So should we fight to stop it,

and stand and shout, "oh stop it".

Not as we examine and gaze,

and shower them with praise.

For the lonely tree amidst the prison of our homes.

So, what of the homes of our allies,

the birds, the bees and butterflies,

who flutter by, and cry,

"Oh, why? Can't you see what's happening?"

Now stare at the future and you will know,

of thick grey air, and land where naught will grow.

And then it is too late,

it will become your fate

and sorrow, unless you make a stand for life.

19 March 1999

MY SWEET CONFESSOR.

Ride again sweet confessor, home.

Your white suit and kind heart

take to, and let them shine like a beacon

up through the villainous stark land.

Go silently without much ado,

and ease into the still darkness,

of a very English Friday morn.

Nothing more true or beautiful.

Swiftly then ride along,

and catch not, the eye or ear

of other night skulkers or early risers.

Then carry with you my loving memory.

THE RISE AND FALL OF THE SACRED TREE

Assassin-like, now you speed

and steel home in haste.

Educate not those who wait for you there,

for love has power but knowledge possesses a greater one.

Seven nights of chastity passed,

I adorn your pale milky flesh.

Then worship your holy face and golden hair once more,

with kisses tender and caresses gentle as a swan's feather.

Lips full of the robin's bright breast,

the brownest of non-shallow eyes,

and the body of the perfect statue,

grace you, with wondrous elegance.

THE RISE AND FALL OF THE SACRED TREE

Beatification eases from me, with happiness

and joy, for love, truly fills my heart.

Madding with adoration, visit again thus I may plea,

ride not again, sweet confessor, home.

JUST ALONE.

Alone I sit,

alone I wait,

for some simple twist of fate.

I was alone until you came,

for me forever,

for you a game.

And now you're gone,

I sit alone,

better for the times I've known.

THE RISE AND FALL OF THE SACRED TREE

WHAT CAN I SEE?

Through the curt triangular gauged eyes,

of the smooth skin and peachy flesh,

I saw deep into the hollow head of a thoughtless creature.

Inside which a powerful light sparked fiercely and burned so

majestically that it captured my attention wholly.

As I looked through the creature,

and stared far into the strong and glorious light,

I became mesmerised by its unique and perfect beauty.

In the distant centre of the light, I saw many wonderful visions

of

love

and total perfection.

After a while I stopped staring into the light.

Then I picked up my pumpkin by its coarse string,

and as I walked around the murky streets clutching it close, on that

chilled October evening so many years ago,

I knew that the amazing light with which I felt so, so safe,

was the light of life,

and it was with me, even then.

THE RISE AND FALL OF THE SACRED TREE

DEATHS LEGACY.

Heroes and villains, in a dateless smokescreen.

Forever in troubled clover, and loved to death

by the Admiral of those magnificent sins.

The jolly man with time on his hands, barks at fools,

who think he is a doctor.

Then turns his back on the very best of his work. He is a vampire of

life's source. He has a legacy, to which everyone must listen.

All hours are watched by he,

all sounds heard, and he withers any whom he wishes, 'tis his whim.

For he knows that young blood will be poured into the

vacant boots of the wise.

He knows tomorrow will don a new unimaginative challenger.

So, he can crumble the silent armies and their sons, but he will toy

with them. He will give newly fledged butterflies a touch of the sun,

       He will...

          He will...

            He will, and

then he will carve them up.

20 December 1998.

DISTANCE.

Distance is a peculiar guest. I woke

this morning to find that he, distance,

had come between us!

Debonair Distance danced like a dream.

Distance paused, asked you to dance,

You did.

Distance, ever dashing, waltzed you across

The polished floor.

Distance, ever eager, then tangoed you

Out the door.

Distance showed another life, he brought you

Different things. He broadened your horizons,

He opened up your wings.

Distance has a brother 'Far-away', his brother's name,

and while Distance made you happy, Far-away made

me the same.

Far-away told me a story. About the years gone by.

He told me about his childhood, he told me the secret

Why…

    He had changed his name.

His real name isn't Far-away, his tale took time

to make sense. His real name isn't Far-away,

his real name, given as he left the womb, is

                                   Absence.

THE RISE AND FALL OF THE SACRED TREE

Absence makes the heart grow fonder, at least

        that's what they say. And certainly, living with

Absence, I feel fonder of you each day.

I know Distance is making you happy,

but his brother is not so much fun.

Maybe if you give Distance the elbow,

we can go back to where we begun.

Distance was always a peculiar guest, debonair

but peculiar,

        and now I find that not only

        are Distance and his brother peculiar,

        But unwelcome too.

1 November 2000

COLD STEEL.

Oh, straight blade, you never looked so pretty to me as you did tonight.

Cold steel, warm and inviting.

I shouldn't be alone with you tonight.

Merry now my curt saviour,

slow pain seems quicker than once it did.

Relieve my sorrow with your honest danger.

Slice jagged, thin, willing flesh,

let light appear upon the trickling rivers of red,

encourage life to ebb away with the cold thick water.

Glisten and menace away heartache and loneliness,

for I shall not arise to clean your silver stillness.

THE RISE AND FALL OF THE SACRED TREE

Thank you, Prince, for opening my last locked door on this night,

and farewell,

for now, who knows when we shall meet again...

SOLEMNESS.

To think alone, knowing inside that all thoughts should be careful and calm.

To know what peace is, and why it should be kept.

To control yourself, against all the odds, no matter what anyone says. Not being concerned about what others think of you.

To live life to its full potential, supporting your role in society. Without having to fulfill other's standards. Not pretending to be something that you can't be, for peers' sakes.

If you can do all of this, being faithful to your soul always.

Then you are someone true, to yourself and everyone,

and I envy you with all that I am.

GUIDE TO A GRITH.

Stringent lampposts guard the roads and slim side streets,

watching over all who stroll down their firm tracks.

Casting down a shadow of false light,

penetrating through the darkness of the night.

When it's I, who walks under their substance,

bathe without thought in yellow downfall.

Not only is it the light, it does bequeath,

it's the tinted air to breathe.

Walk tall then, nothing can lurk in the dark,

No one can pursue you through the beams.

Hold steady, a colour-filled lung of breath,

and stand proud upon that isopleth.

THE RISE AND FALL OF THE SACRED TREE

Take with you courage, wherever you go,

do not waver in any place.

For on this atlas people will always assist,

and protect you against any nematocyst.

Now you have grown and fear nothing,

knowing there is no need to fight alone.

Close by somewhere will be kith,

willing always, to provide a grith.

20 April 1998

REALISATION OF BLINDNESS.

Don't give up yet,

don't give up the fight,

I saw you today and thought that you might.

I felt from your heart,

all the pain that you'd hid,

when you slipped off the path with an oily skid.

Now you are lost,

can't seem to find your way back.,

I wish I were able to guide to the track.

I'd taken for granted,

the lion's strength you were losing,

hiding your fears and showing no bruising.

THE RISE AND FALL OF THE SACRED TREE

Half tears in your eyes,

you seem so close to the edge,

teetering on such a dangerous ledge.

Please be strong,

because I'm sure that you will,

find your way over this mountainous hill.

So don't give up yet,

don't give up the fight,

keep battling 'til the sainted are in your sight.

THE AWAKENING TO THE PROMISED LAND.

Lying there absolutely still, except for the rhythmic raising and lowering of a stomach with feeble arms wrapped uncomfortingly around.

Mesmerised by the tragedy.

The bitter, salty tears pausing on odd taste buds before plummeting on to the already sodden weave of cotton, my second skin.

Paralysed in body and mind.

Listen to the bells, the music, the echoing sounds of silent sadness.

Wave your last knowing goodbye, through the thousands of

black diamonds that restrict your view.

Stumble back unnoticed to your resting place.

I will watch helpless:

I know that you are alive,

I know how I feel,

I know what I want to say,

I know what I need to do,

I don't know what's stopping me!

I'm frightened of that truth,

of your feared truth,

but can we carry on, empty shells, not trying.

I urge you to struggle, to battle, to raise up and beg and plea for love, friendship, work, play, an existence.

But I know that you are losing,

and I am withering away from inside you.

But you, we, us together can strive to take that first

unreachable, learning, growing step.

So others who are forced to follow the same daunting track,

can retrace our footprints in the snow and sand and through the

long grass.

They will take another leap from ours and although we may not

get where we long to go.

We will begin to forge a path, so no others will have to suffer

pain, anguish and isolation like ours.

Eventually, if no one stops trying,

we will reach that paradise with them, in them, and through them,

we will, together.

COULD IT BE!

Reunited, young drummer with no frills,

together with nobody.

Tasteless sour sensations wriggle unlovingly upon your plump

pink tongue,

Bullets of earthy sound, glide like carelessly angry bees

swarming swiftly around your ears,

and your head teeters with many millions of threatening

thoughts that cramp each compartment.

Slump alone in the rigid chair and sip your vodka and lemonade

to console your cowardice.

Tomorrow may be a new day but will it hold any surprise for a

silent speaker?

THE RISE AND FALL OF THE SACRED TREE

Learn from the new book of knowledge,

then let the assorted catastrophes of the past remain buried.

Replace the half-drunken glass of semi-precious liquid,

and regret or pity not, the contorted fortune that fate has dealt for you.

So once again you may be reunited young drummer,

with your life.

ANGEL FACE.

I wish I had someone to love,

with angel face from skies above.

To hold them close, to hold them dear,

secure and happy, no more fear.

From them a love so deep I'd feel,

a love so true, a love so real.

With arms around me, a grip so tight,

holding me each and every night.

With them alone I'd be content,

companionship that's heaven sent.

Alas but they are only dreams,

alone forever, or so it seems.

23 July 1998

WHO?

Slanted demon creep closer towards me

with your thick grey coat wrapped tight,

a right arm lowered and swinging pendulum-like,

Terror of hell arise to fright.

Why do you arrive to torture my flesh?

With a yellow-toothed grin,

watch me and every move I make,

be sure I commit no sin.

Who are you beneath your skull?

Do thoughts of pity hide there somewhere.

If they do, persist not in my pain,

and leave me to grasp fresh breaths of air.

Turn the chase and I'll seek you,

make you flee from this place,

and then uncertain beckon you back,

in order to rest the space.

THE RISE AND FALL OF THE SACRED TREE
THE GRACE OF THE GUN GUISE.

Is the smooth coldness of a barrel not better doubled?

Leant against the wall, creates ease to find,

so can be lightly retrieved with care, when troubled

thoughts leap impishly through a closed off mind.

Look not into that path of sharp stones and darkness, dear

Sir.

An outstretched finger may curl along a slim enemy.

Displaced shoulder pressure stands symmetrically grounded.

Condemned by oneself and, outrageous gentle infamy

creeps like a stranger's evil shadow with intentions

unfounded.

Listen not to the howl and piercing screech of the brains

night sounds, good Sir.

Pulled, pulled without regret or consideration of listening,

the echoes clap, now steadily unpretentiously fades to hum.

Deep, the rich thick carmine pool sits with sun glistening.

No playing harp, for the angel's home, would now

misbecome.

Fear not of the warm sunken place that you visit now, and

alone, beloved Sir.

THE RISE AND FALL OF THE SACRED TREE

TO BECOME.

A small brown seed, that fits in the hand,

can grow into something so tall and so grand.

Man can flourish and grow like the tree,

to strive, to become, whatever he'll be.

You must grab all your chances, with a fist so tight,

and firmly hold on, with all your might.

To become what you want must depend on you,

and can be affected by all that you do.

In life you must try for the best of a start,

hold on to your dreams with all your heart.

The tale is alas behold and low,

try for your best, and never let go.

THE RISE AND FALL OF THE SACRED TREE
GYRATORY POTENTIAL.

When I have died,

I should have tried,

all I wanted to.

The message here,

states very clear,t'That all you want to, do.

You must do your best,

and never rest,

until what's sought is yours.

Then live in rife,

because in this life,

you must open your own doors.

Live not in fear,

from laughter or jeer,

care not what others think.

In body and mind,

THE RISE AND FALL OF THE SACRED TREE

you must seek to find,

your life's own missing link.

So when you're dead,

the words I've said,

will stop you looking back.

You'll say with pride,

I didn't hide,

and my life didn't lack.

THINKING OF YOU.

When the slow songs play at the end of the night.

I think of you.

The ballads – they seem to be our tune. Though you don't know it yet.

The slow love songs, I think. The one's that have the expressive, cautious melody. The sort with the sentences, I only wished that I could say to you. The heart felt lyrics, the wrenching words which can speak things, that only the brave can dream of uttering.

When those slow songs play at the end of the night, and I stand alone in a rapidly emptying club, I think of you.

THE RISE AND FALL OF THE SACRED TREE

And those ballads echo as the last drunken few stagger by, and I watch them listening to our tune. I stand thinking of you, and listen to our music, though you're not with me, and though you still don't know that it's ours, yet.

AND LOVE.

Destiny is a howling dog – which bites you in the morning, then drags you into the uncertainty of the dusk.

Fate is a gurgling toad – which cackles in your ear through the winter, then furnishes you with gifts in the spring.

Luck is a cross-eyed blackbird – which pecks your ankles while you are barefooted, and makes you jump for protection into the nearest pair of shoes, (however ill fitting).

And love.

Love is simply an illness – it can cause the heights of happiness, and the burn of despair. Either way it is the only thing, which no one would be without, and it is the only thing which follows a path from which you can not deviate. The paths are dark and love, love is the vast hole that you fall down while on your way to a totally different dream.

HUNGER.

Consciousness swept over me in the night, when I woke to find you not there.

Then the pain of my wounds highlighted my daze.

I felt the gauges in my heart from where your talons had released me.

Released me, and left me hanging alone in a loose web of blunt despair.

Dangling in a chain of choice – a chain where I was the weakest link.

It was you who kept me strong and able to hold on to the swinging pendulum of hope.

I threw away the time spent on you. It was wasted time – but the minutes tasted so good that I didn't notice.

Now though – I'm hungry – starved of you beauty and embraces, and my arms wait unfolded. Ready to receive the flavour of your love back in my withering heart.

I'm waiting for your sustenance – for your nourishment, ready and forever waiting.

I know though that I shall perish from starvation.

THE RISE AND FALL OF THE SACRED TREE
KNOW WHERE I'M GOING?

Immune to the swarm of the crowd,

I stagger along without pace.

And though their bustle's so loud,

I keep both my track and my pace.

I'm sure of my path, where I'm going.

There's a light that I'm sure I can reach.

And though sometimes doubt may be showing,

you'll not tell a thing from my speech.

For all of my words exit strongly.

They hit target ears like a shot.

And though sometimes I say things quite wrongly,

I wriggle out of the mess on the spot.

THE RISE AND FALL OF THE SACRED TREE

Then if I walk by my goal in this lifetime,

I'll throw all my luck in a pan.

And though my cooking is really a crime,

I shall bake a contingency plan.

TORMENTED TIME.

Every second, a long-lasting thought,

every minute, your mind pulled taught,

waiting for something, anything, nothing.

No time passes by without stuff in your brain,

thoughts that burn, and fill you with pain,

waiting for the eternal torment to cease.

Loneliness aches in your heart like a twisted knife,

forever unseen, but controlling all life,

oh, if only the knife were to do its job properly.

Today as I sat, and inside me plotted,

to work loose the ties of a brain turned knotted,

the coward way out, a coward am I?

THE RISE AND FALL OF THE SACRED TREE

A gun would work, no chance to miss,

from their lips I yearned to drink, just one kiss,

heads turned sideways, eyes focused elsewhere.

Thoughts of you, from them, not there,

in cruel hearts surely lie some, but where,

oh, the ache, still heart bound.

For them you love, you feel and care,

but for you, it hides deep elsewhere.

From you, rejected, feelings cast aside.

Life true, is a bitter pill,

forever the climb of a steep-sloped hill,

life feared the pill is one of different sorts, woefully

swallowed.

THE RISE AND FALL OF THE SACRED TREE
SPEAKING IN AN ACCENT.

Faun lies speak softly through clenched teeth.

Splintering enamel, chips away, eroded in both your faces.

Miserable bitch, with face of ivory, and brain of mushy

globules.

Paint your picture, and drive away in the races.

Something clicks in my mind like a sore watch.

I know you are its source, mind of musical creeping.

Like a Picasso painting, but not as pretty, your dual features

keep on smiling and sickeningly seeping, out.

Go far away, to a distance that nobody knows.

Where your pathetic smarm and grin are well hid.

THE RISE AND FALL OF THE SACRED TREE

Take note that you were forced to leave, and take your

talentless, worthless, A-frame buttocks with you.

After all, you're still a proud, dull kid.

Cross me not again, to my face or behind my turned back.

For I have friendly ears everywhere, not willing to hear you

spout non-sensical tales.

So when you arrive on Monday morning, happy like everything

has been forgotten, - get lost !

Keep faithful to your idiocy, don't be shocked, and remain

festeringly stale.

DUSTY SUNSET.

Dusty sunrise, red and warm,

with grace your orb appears.

Then coats us with a golden balm,

tan, brown, with films of dry dust.

Dusty midday, dry the air,

scorch the grass and leaves.

Rays beam down with panache and flare,

when your crooked smile hits the ground.

Dusty sunset, fade away,

scurry back into your burrow.

Mark with stars the end of day,

and bid greetings to your pale cresented brother.

TIRED HANDS.

I glanced down at my hands this morning and I didn't recognise them. Perhaps I was still half-asleep, but I didn't recognise them.

They were far larger than I remember them to be. Far wider and rougher.

The worn hands of an old man – worn and tired.

They had been overworked, used too much and burnt out. They had been forced to do work which they disliked, work which tired them too easily.

I glanced down at my hands this morning and I didn't recognize them. Perhaps I was still half-asleep, but I washed them with the emerald soap anyway.

COMING HOME.

I opened one eye at first and when the cold stone lion beamed a familiar smile, - I opened the other. Weary from the two days of driving I wasn't sure. Ribbons of tired tears distorted my reality – but I knew that I was home.

Back in the city.
Back where the charcoal sky was flecked with sweet clouds.
Back where a million lights each told a story.
Back.

People were laughing as they left the theatre, remembering a humour-filled line – and loosening clothing as they chortled.

Familiarity squeaked at me with a happy daze, - and the phrase "Home sweet home" suddenly meant something. Something indescribably warming.

It was then that I knew, I knew I was merely twenty minutes from home.

The corners came faster, and recognition stood firm in each road curve and street name.

THE RISE AND FALL OF THE SACRED TREE

The bristling hedges had put on a display of carmine poppies while I'd been away - and the frayed fields' boundaries nestled them in an ocean of ripe wheat. I was home.

I could smell the fading aroma of the day's sun, and then, when I saw how filled with happiness I had become – to see my house amid an army of others, all fighting to reach the horizon and hold onto it.

I knew then that it is more than just the house that makes a home.

So, no matter where I may find myself, some slice of my heart would forever remain here, in the sapphire of the counties.

THE RISE AND FALL OF THE SACRED TREE
STAR DRENCHED THUNDER.

Every time I hear the cry,

Of star-drenched thunder in the sky,

I pause a while, and as I wait.

I know that delusions have taken the bait.

Perhaps ill luck, perhaps just fate.

Love and peace turn sour and hard.

Like a stained red feather from a slaughtered dove.

The good of an age has gone from my head.

The hollow words sing vicious – life is dead.

The blood wine is drunk, and broken is the bread.

The green lawn browns, the leaves plunge desperately.

What can I do now – a skeleton of mystery.

So I'll kneel and cringe – a face of fear.

THE RISE AND FALL OF THE SACRED TREE

Shout and wail hoping someone hears.

On dead ears it falls, on dry ground the tears.

A situation vacant, a special position to be filled.

I'll squat upon a bare wood shelf.

Coping with the dread of dread.

Gaggles of patterns corrupt my head.

Death steals your emotions but leaves your soul instead.

THE RISE AND FALL OF THE SACRED TREE

PLEASE THINK OF ME.

You've gone away, forever you say.

You left at two, at two today.

You "won't come back", but soon we'll see,

don't cry today, please think of me.

You've run away, who knows where?

Filled with anger and a "I don't care".

You parted with huffs and a fiddle de de.

Don't cry today, please think of me.

Paris, London, Venice or Rome,

off in search of a nice new home.

To travel the world, the sights to see.

Don't cry today, please think of me.

THE RISE AND FALL OF THE SACRED TREE

A house, apartment, tent or flat,

in an upturned box or discarded hat.

Wherever you are – in tent or tepee,

don't cry today, please think of me.

I'll roll my dice and wish you luck,

hope you feel free from my unbaited hook.

Then I'll say it again, wherever you be,

don't cry today, please think of me.

SECRETS OF THE DARK.

Arriving with care, your eyes hold a story,

of passion and pride and fearless glory.

Don't tell me please, the secret strong,

I want not to know what you have done wrong.

My mind will rest, free of that stain,

if you hide me from the certain pain.

Keep me secluded and in the dark,

keep me liberated of a bruise or mark.

THE RISE AND FALL OF THE SACRED TREE

Although without scar, the torment I feel,

is still so harsh and rough and real.

The truth of yours from which I hide,

is melting me from deep inside.

Smile to me recall my ease,

beckon with a happy please.

Then I'll bury my thoughts in a place I'll find,

in the darkest corner of my mind.

WATERY EYES.

I washed my face in the brilliant gleam of a silvery star,
and the strange and strong sensation blew me to a far-off diamond-encrusted mountain.
My mountain, upon which I sat head high in the soft, dank clouds.

I looked far down at a frothing river flowing wildly with true harshness.
The river had many twists and turns, and forked in many places along it's course,
and on the river I saw a small boat battling against the fierce waters.

I knew immediately that the river was a symbol of my life,
and it was me on the boat battling,
struggling for a pure existence.

So, from where I sat, from high up on my mountain,
I could see that if I chose the right path along the waters of my life,
that the river was straight and calm, and that all of my goals could be reached.

I feel so sure that there is a similar tale for each of us.

It's a horrible pity, the saddest thing in the world that we don't know it, and so few of us fight the fiery waters that hold us back,

from achieving what we really and truly want,

with all that we are..!

THE RISE AND FALL OF THE SACRED TREE

DAYS, DAYS, DAYS.

Days will come, and days will go.

Once they've left what can we show.

Normal days will fly so fast,

happy days will hardly last.

Can anyone see the days I know.

Today was almost in every way,

more perfect than even words can say.

I felt a pride, I've never felt,

I received a hand, I've never been dealt.

Yet something still eluded this day.

THE RISE AND FALL OF THE SACRED TREE

For days are brief, and gone too soon.

Time ticks fast when lovers swoon.

So, hold onto memories in your mind,

keep them fresh, with joy to find.

Colour thoughts on a pale, dry day.

In a circle, days come around,

and so I've nearly always found,

when mistakes are made, don't fret and fear,

tomorrow a new day will sure appear.

A day within which, you'll make a contented sound.

27 January 1999

PERSPECTIVE

Knotting, splitting, kissing, blessing.

Rotting, sitting, missing, dressing.

Bloodletting – losing,

Slanting – bruising,

Biting – confusing,

Grieving – amusing.

Distracted by the mouth-watering morsels

of

flavouring – perishing.

Distant, birth, unfurnished, death,

Insistent, worth, unfinished, breath.

Idealistic – sceptic,

Realistic – septic.

THE RISE AND FALL OF THE SACRED TREE

The migrating ducks form an arrow

shadowing through the sky,

Aiding you through the seaweed.

Stopping you from treading on the washed

up starfish – scry.

Beg for a slug of a dreg from a jug.

Replenish the blood, call it back, and tell it

Why and how much you love it.

                      Convince it you do,

                            You do,

                      Do you? Don't you…?

The small overdone monkey you eat as you

run is still alive.

Thinking of a tablespoon of thick nectar –

dreaming of a honeymoon on

THE RISE AND FALL OF THE SACRED TREE

A soon June noon, in a moonlit dune.

Content.

Dormant ducks still glide, your attachment continues.

Adamant in your enjoyment you still follow.

The sands of time end curtly.

Look out over the precipice into the never ending

blue blackness. It is dark, stale and starless.

Night, sight, half-light, backbite,

Plight, flight, fight, frostbite.

File the depths, the heights – with lights.

THE RISE AND FALL OF THE SACRED TREE

A starfish waits before you. You lift it and

Caress it. You fell the dying suction of its

Arms stroking your fingers – making love

to them.

Blood pressure heightens in your muscles

as you arch

Back your sapling arm – launching the star –

Discus like – into the sky.

The lake of air rejuvenates it, it breathes

again.

It swims and spins like a snowflake

swooping

Through the shipwreck of space.

Blacksnake, flee, darkness, see,

Opaque, plea, frameless, free.

THE RISE AND FALL OF THE SACRED TREE

In those fathoms, of gas, the starfish which

Has lived before, lives again.

From the sure shore visibility confirms

That your pentacle is now the brightest of

                          Them

  All.

1 November 2000

THE RISE AND FALL OF THE SACRED TREE
P.O.W.

An angel born on earth, to perform a prophetic role,

who strived to give, to create a paradise for all.

You filled with love and tenderness each hollow, empty soul,

and took any into your arms, no matter how old or small.

We watched as you exploded with an independent spirit,

dragged us from clasped horrors of agony and despair,

so, with rich heart and soft word you gave inspirit,

with vibrations of strength, from you, gentle carillonneur.

You rang through us with passion and with pride,

displaced with us your quiet power,

drifted in, now leave like the wayward tide,

still, you upturn the thoughts that make minds sour.

THE RISE AND FALL OF THE SACRED TREE

It's with a lump in our throat that we say goodbye,

on us all you cast a magical spell,

not a single person has a fresh cheek or dry eye,

as we bid you our final farewell.

September 1997

LIES?

Is it lies that hurt so much?

Their rough and deathly, stabbing touch!

And from the lies that you are told,

your spine will shiver freezing cold.

Is it lies that burn so deep,

that cause you to cry and scream and weep?

So when you're lying on the floor,

and yell out loud, I want no more -

is it lies that bring you round,

that pull you gently from the ground?

And comfort and care and dry your tears,

then reassure you from your fears.

THE RISE AND FALL OF THE SACRED TREE

Is it lies that then, drops you like concrete gold,

to fall so far through your world, it shatters your very mold.

Once more ask the question you clutch,

is it lies that hurt so much?

THE RISE AND FALL OF THE SACRED TREE
AN ODE TO A DISTANT MEMORY.

I'm so lonely,

no one can seem to understand,

my false smile will hide everything,

he still has the upper hand.

Does he really know how I'm feeling?

I realise what I explained was wrong,

can the smile mask all that's inside,

because the love for him remains so strong.

Why have I been denied,

of all the love he cannot feel,

my hearts churned to a thousand pieces,

that's how much you steal.

What I'd do to be with him,

to be able to feel his touch,

but, I can't do a single thing,

though I need him so much.

He would say I'm attractive,

every word was a lie,

he didn't love me at all, I think,

he longed to say goodbye.

I still care so much,

I just can't seem to let go,

I feel so destroyed inside,

I can't allow my unhappiness to show.

THE RISE AND FALL OF THE SACRED TREE

I thought that I'd discovered my life,

with someone I love.

my head won't absorb all this,

tormented by the shove.

I wish that I could kiss those lips,

whispering the words that need to be said,

I wish it could be easy,

I need to know the thoughts that fill his head.

He tells me, he's not good enough,

but I love the way he is.

he tells me, that it can't be love,

but I know it is.

THE RISE AND FALL OF THE SACRED TREE

Whenever my eyes see him,

my heart will skip a beat,

it's a battle between both our hearts,

and mine will show defeat.

There are a million words

I only wish that I could say.

It's hard to cope with the way that I feel,

and see him day after day.

I wish we could be together.

I know we could see it through,

one day soon, I'll show him this....

I love you.

11 October 1997

THE RISE AND FALL OF THE SACRED TREE

YESTERDAY WAS A LONG TIME AGO.

I'm always told there are more fish in the sea,

but I just can't learn to swim.

I'll stand on the shore, forever alone,

thinking of life with him.

My recollections of your face are fading dim.

Though in my thoughts I still kiss your soft lips,

my fingertips can still feel the grain of your cheeks,

I still smell the freshness of your hair on every breath,

and I can still, still see the smile that you held deep in your bright eyes.

I'm thankful to every wiser power, for the few days

spent with you, and not angry because now you're gone.

Not angry. Desolated, destroyed, and shuddering from terror, but not angry, not angry at all.

Sit me solitary again, in a lonely spot. Tremors and tears

pause on the recollection of every soft word you spoke.

Did I tell you, did I show you enough? - No. No, no.

I let you slip through my weak net, couldn't I have

tried harder to preserve something wonderful. I know

that it's my fault that you're gone.

Countdown to when the presents of regret and remembrance,

flee to leave warm, smiling, joyful tears of tinted memories.

Man will always love more, the one who refuses to love him.

19 October 1997

TOMORROWS TREPIDATION.

I stared deep into the eyes of an ageing sorrow filled man,

he looked back in dismay at me, the crows feet creeping ever more around his eyes.

The shallow wrinkles fell into place upon his tired skin, creased like a slept-on blanket.

Where had the young boy gone, the one whose place has been quietly stolen?

The face of youth has slipped away unnoticed, and the ageing man peers back in panic.

The waters silver skin shows, what spoken words hide.

Why has yesterday gone, slid away in silence, tomorrow arrives unannounced, and filters into a year of sprightly time.

When did the days become minutes, when I stared deep into the eyes of an ageing sorrow filled man.

I stared in disbelief, I stared.

I stared at my tomorrow, I stared.

27 November 1998

THE RISE AND FALL OF THE SACRED TREE
OPPOSITE TOADS MOUTH.

Flat, hard, rough, slender.

Discrete squelches surround

the inanimate, obsolete

fragments of Lawrence's Field.

Surrounded, guarded, protected,

watched, waited on,

imprisoned, held, bound,

loved, caressed, enveloped, suffocated.

Unearthed, uncovered, found,

discovered, inspected, scrutinised,

touched, felt, words that melt,

loved, caressed, enveloped… suffocated.

THE RISE AND FALL OF THE SACRED TREE

Left, stranded, depleted, drained,

dried, desiccated, dissipated.

Uncovered, unearthed, unprotected.

uncaring squelches slap around

the fragile archaic

fragments of Lawrence's Field.

13 October 2000

THE RISE AND FALL OF THE SACRED TREE
FROM THE CROSSBEAM.

To and fro,

they come and go.

Smile while leaving,

conceal the grieving.

Shut their eyes,

from shock or surprise.

Cold, they feel,

away, they steal.

How to pretend

my life would well mend

if they would just end

my solitude.

THE RISE AND FALL OF THE SACRED TREE

How to pretend?

All I need is a friend,

with a heart they would lend,

but they don't.

So what to do now?

Stop asking me how!

How will I cope?

Released from the rope?

I don't know!

Can't let go!

What I've lost I'll regain,

then umbrella the rain.

THE RISE AND FALL OF THE SACRED TREE

I will breathe air once more,

I will drop to the floor,

I will scream out and roar,

cut me free…!

No one can hear!

Me, alone with my fear,

draped like a tear,

from a towrope.

13 October 2000

THE RISE AND FALL OF THE SACRED TREE

COUGHING.

Digesting rubble with a sponge-lined stomach.

The thoughts convulse your muscles, with

repulsion and shock from the slimy, grimy

crunching sliding foaming gravel, lining pink flesh.

Spying you, coughing up grit, swallowing

the stone, regaining your composure and

smiling through pain.

You are brave for us, we reciprocate your

façade. We worsen your obligations – your

Britishness - your maleness.

Chalk chokes, sandstone erodes your touch.

Lime weighs – levelling your calcium. Fossilising

your skeleton, turning you to coal – on

which you gag.

Spluttering on the unspoken word, shattering

into fragments and slivers the stone that

shapes your heart.

Sediment has fallen to the bottom of your

mind and now it won't be moved.

Settling particles cement the flakes that

fell before, forcing destiny, because you

won't shelter,

won't speak,

won't live.

31 October 2000

THE RISE AND FALL OF THE SACRED TREE

THE TALE THE TREE COULD HAVE TOLD.

We sat beneath the chestnut tree,

sat staring at the sun.

You and me together, free,

a romance just begun.

In the sky pale clouds were hydrated,

but held back their storm for us.

Flying insects hummed and celebrated,

birds swooped and made such a fuss.

The dark night soon began falling,

not totally alone in its descent.

As we parted, your heart went on calling,

mine skipped, when received what you sent.

THE RISE AND FALL OF THE SACRED TREE

Through the hours of night, of you I dreamt,

of what I so longed to say.

But hours became weeks, and so it sempt,

an eternity until the next day.

When we finally met and I saw you,

in the park, on that sunny day.

I held you so tight and I told you,

exactly what I wanted to say.

I opened my heart, told my feelings,

your words hit me back with a smack.

You said, you hoped I'd start healing,

you were going and not coming back.

THE RISE AND FALL OF THE SACRED TREE

You turned and left me alone there,

alone with my pain and my hurt.

It was so plain to see that you didn't care,

from the words that were destroyingly curt.

From that day to this, you've vanished,

and now I don't care what you do.

My only wish, is that where you've been banished,

some pain of mine lingers with you.

THE UNKNOWN.

What do you see when you look at me,

when you look into my eyes?

The same strong person I used to be,

a lifeless ordinary, with no surprise?

But look inside where love should dwell,

an empty chasm lies.

Is only filled with the pain of hell,

in a strong but subtle guise.

My stern brave face alas no good,

to me there feels no love.

My heart pumps tears in place of blood,

and fits me like a glove.

THE RISE AND FALL OF THE SACRED TREE

The outer shell that's surrounding me,

and hides me from the world.

Is breaking down so all can see,

I hurt when things are hurled.

And when they look but are so blind,

to see what's going on.

Not feel the turmoil in my mind,

and peace, of which there's none.

I scream inside and no one hears,

the horror in my heart.

That I'm alone and no one cares,

as I slowly fall apart.

THE RISE AND FALL OF THE SACRED TREE

Give me a sign please, a glimmer of hope,

as it drags me just below.

Share the strength to battle, the will to cope,

and please don't let me go.

Through the dark and baron land,

carry me along.

Pull me up and clasp my hand,

together we'll be strong.

Then when the fires dampened down,

the troubles passed away.

Eases off my sorrowed frown,

for the hope of another day.

THE RISE AND FALL OF THE SACRED TREE

So next time when you look at me,

I hope you'll learn to start.

Open your eyes and begin to see,

the sorrow in my heart.

A FRIEND IN NEED.

Someone who listens with a helping ear,

and always will be there.

Who knows your faults,

and what you're like,

and still for you they care.

When problems arise and get you down,

they try to pull you through.

No matter what,

the baron land,

they're always there for you.

THE RISE AND FALL OF THE SACRED TREE

A friend like this is true and good,

their heart is made with gold,

So never forget,

to repay their kind,

when troubles for them unfold.

MELANCHOLY MOTHER.

No wind in the trees,

no waves on the sand,

all over, this world is a desolate land.

It's not Mother Nature,

or what she has done,

it's man in his element, and having such fun.

No cares for the future,

just here and now,

together we'd stop it, but we all allow.

Think of our children,

the future to come,

in a world of distorted beauty, and beat on by the sun.

THE RISE AND FALL OF THE SACRED TREE

It's the job of all that are living,

to strive without failure or mirth,

to know why our earth is so precious, and exactly just what it

is worth.

Care and protect it whole hearted,

whether you're strong or you're meek.

Don't let it become how it started,

Unmanaged, uncared for and bleak...

FRUIT FOR THOUGHT.

With eager patience, we wait.

Watching its still bareness through the winter,

with its blanket of soft pure snow settled carefully on its branches.

My father used to say that the snow was there to protect our tree, because it had lost its leaves.

I always felt that we were stealing from nature each time we burnt large piles of its multicoloured leaves, through the autumn months.

But every spring it started, like a well-oiled car.

From the tip of each twig and branch it burst with buds and blossom.

Then fought against the purple, peach and white crocus to form fully-fledged flowers.

Yet when competing had done, and the faded flowers of the crocus lay limp on the lawn, the flowers of our tree changed and formed into plump, round, rosy apples that bathed daily in the gentle heat of the summer sun.

Later we picked them carefully and placed them on old

crumpled newspapers, which protected them until they were needed.

As a boy, I always remember that each apple that I selected and ate, was filled with the summer days in which they had grown.

So, as I sat through the bleakest of winters and stared out upon our apple tree, holding the half-eaten fruit in my hands,

I was warmed with all the joys of summer and all the memories of spring.

THE MIRROR OF TRUTH.

Mirror, mirror, looking back at me,

so deep inside what do you see?

Dislodged hopes and desires?

Your unpretentious truth tells not a lie,

when it sees the reflection of tears in my eye.

Realisation of defeat can crush!

As the face before you ages years,

you change your angle, conceal your fears.

Wisdom grows for each wrinkle.

Slowly I realise that we're all the same,

in poverty, wealth, obscure or in fame.

Your honesty will burn us all.

THE RISE AND FALL OF THE SACRED TREE

We all have a goal; we all have that dream,

life is never all peaches and cream.

And you know it so well.

Although you're not cruel, your honesty prevails,

and plainly displays, to us all how we fail.

Cornered by truth and doubt we will fall.

OCTOBER THE SECOND, NINETEEN HUNDRED AND NINETY-NINE.

Last night when you spoke to me I was

engergised again – though for the first time

everything that I needed to say to you, you said to me!

Courageousness left me momentarily, but you found it.

Opened up everything, which was lodged within me.

Of all the things I wanted from the second of October, I

could never have dreamt for more than this.

Presumptuousness probably overtakes me – though I hope

not. Even carefully scripted poetry can't begin to capture what I wished it would.

Read it through - and know this, perhaps "like" is just not a

strong enough word.

THE RISE AND FALL OF THE SACRED TREE
A FACE IN THE MUD.

Nestling in the mud a shape lay – an outline.

Patterned splashes of grime and red adorned the form.

He was fodder, faceless, a number. Though a comrade of mine –

a comrade. Shoulder to shoulder – we marched as a swarm.

The squelch of clinging filth and the silent whistle still deafen me,

I closed my eyes and ran to him, discovered yet half buried.

Unearthing his face snow melted from my eyes and I could no longer see.

Frosted vision and a limp soul now ebbed and are ferried.

Slapping boots ran past, sliding toward a fate,

Sipping in the cup of an iced sunset. Blue and final.

Stuck in a memory of distant reality, brimming with loss and gnawing hate.

Slipping into the ocean of an iced sunset. Blue and final.

His chilled expression mirrored still his battle cry, his cry.

Squalid gold said his end would be well mourned too.

As the advancing enemy of dark vacuuming coldness eased by,

We sat together gazing at ghosts and I watched him. Final and blue.

THE RISE AND FALL OF THE SACRED TREE
ANCHORED IN THE RAIN.

Black lightning stings the fat clouds.

With my head anchored back I can see,

their brawl; and it's cold here in the shadows of your heart.

I knew from the start it wouldn't be easy – but I tried, regardless.

I wore your ribbon and sang your song,

and though I continued in my attempts, you quit.

You hit fifty and gave up.

Fifty miles an hour an hour on a thin B road,

you gave up and turned back.

Headed for home and left me wondering where you were.

Now I know where you are –

Where black lightning stings the fat clouds, where I can see you.

Where it's cold, it is cold isn't it?

WORDS OF WORTH.

Oh inspiration divine,

like cool fresh water that lies unstirred at the very bottom of

a mountain stream.

Creep quietly into my mind as would a silent visitor,

who seeks me to whisper dishonest truths upon my ignorant

ear.

So, command my mind and hand to write the monster that

you have created through me.

Your used and unimaginative words twist themselves until

contorted into a deformed sentence of no worth.

Which will lie disgracefully on an ugly page.

Wasted ink writes you and ruined paper receives you,

you and your natural foulness.

Stay there mute,

then let not searching eyes see you in your glorious day of

destruction.

THE RISE AND FALL OF THE SACRED TREE
THE DEMON'S DUTY.

Hippocras, hippocras, hippocras, so who will cry the words

to cast a spell of happiness,

on ears of despair,

that live only to quench the constant crave of sweetly

muttered sounds.

Should you not distort the syllables and scream the noise of

what has been written,

for your chance to do what is truly your destiny,

grows ever nearer and faster than you can crush the aching

screeches out,

from the vast deep chasm that dwells so far in the heart of

your soul.

Speak and be free,

say the burning words and as each one escapes,

feel relief for now you will have fulfilled your ultimate fate,

and rest,

in momentary peace.

CITIZEN Z.

Cracking tremors click and crick their darting path, through volumes of thought.

Balancing amidst a crowd of surging, soundless, faceless entities.

I spin in their swirl - unnoticed.

I spin and spin and spin - unnoticed.

They all maneuver their quickening swirl, with determination and conviction. Static I am unnoticed purposely by their personal glee.

Nervous uncomfortable smiles rush past me.
They dart and fly and rush past me.

And I try so hard, not to care what people think, or say to me.

I try so hard, not to be chilled or scorched by careless whispers and secluded smirks.

But they scar me in other ways.

They pinch and twist and pull and grab and scar me, in other ways.

That barely show upon my dying shell, save tired eyes longing for sleep, and a frowning smile.

The night is the worst, when the swirl has faded and the dreams come.

THE RISE AND FALL OF THE SACRED TREE

The terrors lurking, the sweat and the dreams come.

Through the dark I live my days again, the swirl, the Loneliness, the smiles again, every second, again.

3 February 1999.

Fiducia in eo quod nondum potes videre.

Printed in Great Britain
by Amazon

9e1d9f21-68d4-4c41-83c1-cd38382554d2R01